Mexican Cookbook

Delicious Mexican Recipes Cook at Home

Louise Wynn

Table of Contents

Homemade Mexican tortilla chips

Ingredients:

- 4 wraps or soft burritos
- Salt
- ½ tsp smoked paprika
- 2 cloves garlic
- 2 Tbs olive oil or spray

Instructions:

Preheat the oven to 200°C

Cut the wraps into small pizza slices (12 triangles per wrap)

Place the triangles onto an oven tray and spread them out evenly, trying not to let them overlap

Crush the garlic cloves through a garlic crusher and spread over the wrap triangles.

Sprinkle the salt and paprika over the triangles.

Finally, drizzle the olive oil over top of the triangles to roughly coat.

Place the tray into the oven to bake for approximately 20 minutes, or until the tortilla chips have crisped up like nacho chips!

Serve as a starter or as your very own homemade chips for nachos.

Chicken tacos

Ingredients:

- 500g chicken breast or thigh
- 1 onion
- 1 clove garlic
- 2 Tbs extra virgin olive oil
- 1 tsp ground smoked or sweet paprika
- ¼ tsp nutmeg
- ¼ tsp ground coriander
- 3 shakes ground cardamom
- ½ tsp ground cumin

- ¼ tsp salt
- 3 shake chili flakes
- 1 400g tin crushed tomatoes
- 1 carrot, grated
- Lettuce, finely chopped
- 1 avocado, sliced
- 1 cup grated cheese
- 1 packet taco shells

Instructions:

Place a medium saucepan on the stove over a medium heat.

Finely dice the onion and garlic, and place into the saucepan with the olive oil.

Brown the onion and garlic in the pan for about 5 minutes or until the onions are translucent and fragrant.

Turn the pan up to a high heat.

Slice the chicken up into very thin strips then place into the pan to brown all over for about 7 minutes.

Add all of the spices and salt to the pan and mix well to coat the chicken.

Fry the spices with the chicken for about 5 minutes.

Lastly, add the can of tomatoes and mix well to combine.

Turn the pan down to a low heat and simmer the chicken for about 15 minutes until it becomes coated in flavoring.

Lay a taco shell on a plate and spoon the chicken inside.

Grate the carrot and cheese, chop the lettuce and avocado and serve these vegetables on top of the chicken in your taco shell and enjoy!

Sweet sticky chicken wings

Ingredients:

- 20 chicken wings
- 3 tbs brown sugar
- 2 tbs runny honey
- ¼ cup soy sauce
- 1 Tbs hoisin sauce
- 1 tsp sesame oil

Instructions:

1. Preheat the oven to 180 and line the large baking tray with baking paper.

2. Combine all of the ingredients (except the chicken) in the large bowl. Mix with a whisk thoroughly for about 2 minutes or until the brown sugar dissolves into the mixture.

3. Place the chicken wings into the sauce mixture and toss around with your hands to ensure the chicken gets a good coating of the sauce.

4. Keep the leftover sauce.

5. Place the chicken onto baking tray, being careful not to overlap the wings, and place into the oven for about 40 minutes, or until cooked and the outside of the chicken is crispy

6. Take the chicken out after 15 minutes and spoon the remaining sticky sauce over top of the chicken. Return the chicken to the oven.

7. Once the chicken is cooked, serve with plain Greek yoghurt as a delicious entree that kids with absolutely love!

Sweet chili Guacamole

Ingredients:

- 3 avocados
- 2 Tbs sweet chili sauce
- 1 clove garlic
- ¼ tsp smoked paprika

Instructions:

Spoon the contents of the avocados out into a small serving bowl

Crush the garlic through a garlic crusher and add to the avocado with the rest of the ingredients.

Mash the ingredients together with a fork until combined, with coarse chunks of avocado still remaining.

Serve this special guacamole with tortilla chips as a fancy Mexican-style entrée.

Chicken burritos

Ingredients:

- 500g chicken breast or thigh
- 1 onion
- 1 clove garlic
- 2 Tbs extra virgin olive oil
- 1 tsp ground smoked or sweet paprika
- ¼ tsp nutmeg
- ¼ tsp ground coriander
- 3 shakes ground cardamom
- ½ tsp ground cumin
- ¼ tsp salt
- 3 shake chili flakes
- 1 400g tin crushed tomatoes
- 1 carrot, grated

- Lettuce, finely chopped
- 1 avocado, sliced
- 1 cup grated cheese
- 1 packet burritos/wraps

Instructions:

Place a medium saucepan on the stove over a medium heat.

Finely dice the onion and garlic, and place into the saucepan with the olive oil.

Brown the onion and garlic in the pan for about 5 minutes or until the onions are translucent and fragrant.

Turn the pan up to a high heat.

Slice the chicken up into very thin strips then place into the pan to brown all over for about 7 minutes.

Add all of the spices and salt to the pan and mix well to coat the chicken.

Fry the spices with the chicken for about 5 minutes.

Lastly, add the can of tomatoes and mix well to combine.

Turn the pan down to a low heat and simmer the chicken for about 15 minutes until it becomes coated in flavoring.

Lay a burrito or wrap on a plate and spoon the chicken on one side of the wrap.

Grate the carrot and cheese, chop the lettuce and avocado and serve these vegetables on top of the chicken.

Roll the burrito up and enjoy!

Chicken nachos

Ingredients:

- 500g chicken breast or thigh
- 1 onion
- 1 clove garlic
- 2 Tbs extra virgin olive oil
- 1 tsp ground smoked or sweet paprika
- ¼ tsp nutmeg
- ¼ tsp ground coriander
- 3 shakes ground cardamom
- ½ tsp ground cumin
- ¼ tsp salt
- 3 shake chili flakes
- 1 400g tin crushed tomatoes
- 1 carrot, grated
- Lettuce, finely chopped
- 1 avocado, sliced
- 1 cup grated cheese

- 1 packet nacho chips

Instructions:

Place a medium saucepan on the stove over a medium heat.

Finely dice the onion and garlic, and place into the saucepan with the olive oil.

Brown the onion and garlic in the pan for about 5 minutes or until the onions are translucent and fragrant.

Turn the pan up to a high heat.

Slice the chicken up into very thin strips then place into the pan to brown all over for about 7 minutes.

Add all of the spices and salt to the pan and mix well to coat the chicken.

Fry the spices with the chicken for about 5 minutes.

Lastly, add the can of tomatoes and mix well to combine.

Turn the pan down to a low heat and simmer the chicken for about 15 minutes until it becomes coated in flavoring.

Grate the cheese.

Serve the chicken on top of a bed of the nacho chips and cover with grated cheese.

Smooth avocado dip

Ingredients:

- 2 avocados
- Juice of 1 lemon
- ¼ cup cashew nuts

Instructions:

1. Spoon the contents of the avocado into a small blender.

2. Add the rest of the ingredients to the blender.

3. Blend the mixture on medium until completely smooth.

4. Serve the avocado dip in a small bowl and serve with nacho chips or carrot sticks for a yummy afternoon snack!

Creamy chili coriander dressing

Ingredient:

- 250ml coconut cream
- ¼ cup plain Greek yogurt
- 1 red chili
- 1 bunch fresh coriander
- 1 clove garlic
- ¼ tsp salt
- ¼ tsp paprika

Instructions:

Finely chop the coriander, garlic and chili

Combine these aromatics with the rest of the ingredients in a small serving bowl.

Mix together thoroughly with a spoon to incorporate

Serve over chicken tacos, or over top of nachos for a fancy twist on sour cream!

Creamy coconut paprika chicken tacos

Ingredients:

- 500g chicken breast or thigh
- 1 onion
- 1 clove garlic
- 2 Tbs extra virgin olive oil
- 1 tsp ground smoked or sweet paprika
- ¼ tsp smoked paprika
- ¼ tsp ground coriander
- ½ tsp ground turmeric
- ½ tsp ground cumin
- ¼ tsp salt
- 3 shake chili flakes
- 300ml coconut cream

- Zest of 1 lemon
- Lettuce, finely chopped
- 1 avocado, sliced
- 1 cup grated cheese
- 1 packet taco shells

Instructions:

Place a medium saucepan on the stove over a medium heat.

Finely dice the onion and garlic, and place into the saucepan with the olive oil.

Brown the onion and garlic in the pan for about 5 minutes or until the onions are translucent and fragrant.

Turn the pan up to a high heat.

Slice the chicken up into very thin strips then place into the pan to brown all over for about 7 minutes.

Add all of the spices and salt to the pan and mix well to coat the chicken.

Fry the spices with the chicken for about 5 minutes.

Lastly, add the coconut cream and mix well to combine.

Turn the pan down to a low heat and simmer the chicken for about 12 minutes in the sauce until it becomes coated in flavoring and orange in color.

Lay a taco shell on a plate and spoon the creamy chicken inside.

Grate the cheese, chop the lettuce and avocado and serve these vegetables on top of the chicken in your taco shell and enjoy!

Tacos

Ingredients:

- 500g beef mince
- 1 onion
- 1 clove garlic
- 2 Tbs extra virgin olive oil
- 1 tsp ground smoked or sweet paprika
- ¼ tsp nutmeg
- ¼ tsp ground coriander
- 3 shakes ground cardamom
- ½ tsp ground cumin
- ¼ tsp salt
- 3 shake chili flakes

- 1 400g tin crushed tomatoes
- 1 carrot, grated
- Lettuce, finely chopped
- 1 avocado, sliced
- 1 cup grated cheese
- 1 packet taco shells

Instructions:

Place a medium saucepan on the stove over a medium heat.

Finely dice the onion and garlic, and place into the saucepan with the olive oil.

Brown the onion and garlic in the pan for about 5 minutes or until the onions are translucent and fragrant.

Turn the pan up to a high heat.

Add all of the beef mince to the pan and brown the mince for about 7 minutes.

Add all of the spices and salt to the pan and mix well to coat the mince.

Fry the spices with the mince for about 5 minutes.

Lastly, add the can of tomatoes and mix well to combine.

Turn the pan down to a low heat and simmer the mince for about 15 minutes until it becomes very soft and broken down.

Lay a taco shell on a plate and spoon the mince inside.

Grate the carrot and cheese, chop the lettuce and avocado and serve these vegetables on top of the mince in your taco shell and enjoy!

Creamy coconut paprika chicken wraps

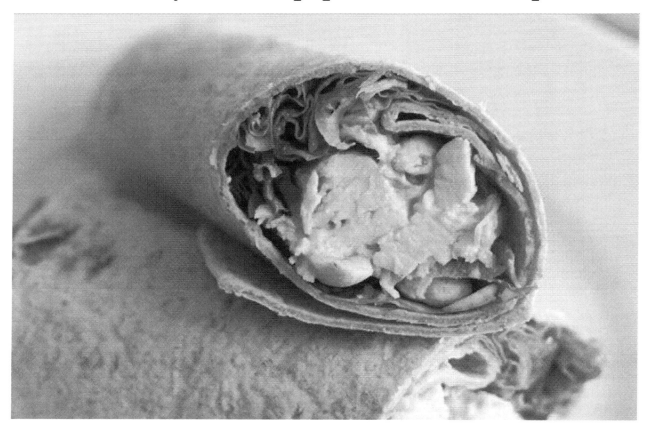

Ingredients:

- 500g chicken breast or thigh
- 1 onion
- 1 clove garlic
- 2 Tbs extra virgin olive oil
- 1 tsp ground smoked or sweet paprika
- ¼ tsp smoked paprika
- ¼ tsp ground coriander
- ½ tsp ground turmeric
- ½ tsp ground cumin
- ¼ tsp salt
- 3 shake chili flakes
- 300ml coconut cream
- Zest of 1 lemon

- Lettuce, finely chopped
- 1 avocado, sliced
- 1 cup grated cheese
- 1 packet wraps or soft burritos

Instructions:

Place a medium saucepan on the stove over a medium heat.

Finely dice the onion and garlic, and place into the saucepan with the olive oil.

Brown the onion and garlic in the pan for about 5 minutes or until the onions are translucent and fragrant.

Turn the pan up to a high heat.

Slice the chicken up into very thin strips then place into the pan to brown all over for about 7 minutes.

Add all of the spices and salt to the pan and mix well to coat the chicken.

Fry the spices with the chicken for about 5 minutes.

Lastly, add the coconut cream and mix well to combine.

Turn the pan down to a low heat and simmer the chicken for about 12 minutes in the sauce until it becomes coated in flavoring and orange in color.

Lay a wrap on a plate and spoon the creamy chicken inside.

Grate the cheese, chop the lettuce and avocado and serve these vegetables on top of the chicken in your wrap, roll them up into a burrito shape and enjoy!

Mexican pork skewers

Ingredients:

- 500g of pork steaks
- A packet of large skewer sticks
- 2 large red capsicums
- 1 tsp smoked paprika
- ¼ tsp ground coriander
- ½ cup Greek yoghurt
- ¼ tsp salt
- ¼ tsp ground cumin
- 2 cloves garlic

Instructions:

1. Crush the garlic through a garlic crusher and add to a large mixing bowl.

2. Place all of the other ingredients into the mixing bowl (except for the capsicum and pork)

3. Mix the sauce thoroughly to combine and set aside.

4. Cut the pork steaks up into medium sized chunks to thread onto the skewers.

5. Cut the capsicum into rough, medium chunks as well.

6. Add the pork chunks to the sauce mixture, and using your hands, toss through the sauce to completely coat the pork in the sauce.

7. Next, thread a piece of pork onto a skewer, then a piece of capsicum, and repeat until you fill up the skewer. Repeat this process until you produce a tray full of pork and capsicum skewers.

8. Heat a large saucepan or grill plate over the stove over a medium heat. Add 4 Tbs of olive oil.

9. Once the pan is hot, add the skewers, a small batch at a time and cook for about 10 minutes - make sure to turn them so that they brown and cook on each side.

10. Serve the skewers with extra Greek yoghurt to dip into and enjoy!

Mince Guacamole

Ingredients:

- 500g beef mince
- 1 onion
- 1 clove garlic
- 2 Tbs extra virgin olive oil
- 1 tsp ground smoked or sweet paprika
- ¼ tsp nutmeg
- ¼ tsp ground coriander
- 3 shakes ground cardamom
- ½ tsp ground cumin
- ¼ tsp salt
- 3 shake chili flakes
- 1 400g tin crushed tomatoes
- 2 avocados
- 1 Tbs sweet chili sauce

Instructions:

Place a medium saucepan on the stove over a medium heat.

Finely dice the onion and garlic, and place into the saucepan with the olive oil.

Brown the onion and garlic in the pan for about 5 minutes or until the onions are translucent and fragrant.

Turn the pan up to a high heat.

Add all of the beef mince to the pan and brown the mince for about 7 minutes.

Add all of the spices and salt to the pan and mix well to coat the mince.

Fry the spices with the mince for about 5 minutes.

Lastly, add the can of tomatoes and mix well to combine.

Turn the pan down to a low heat and simmer the mince for about 15 minutes until it becomes very soft and broken down.

Meanwhile, mash both avocados up in a bowl with the sweet chili sauce to produce a smooth, yet still slightly coarse guacamole.

Serve the mince in a bowl and top with the freshly made guacamole for a gluten and rice free meal option!

Corn on the cob with pistachio cream dip

Ingredients:

- 4 x whole corn on the cob
- 4 Tbs butter
- ½ cup sour cream
- ¼ cup pistachio kernels
- Salt pepper to taste
- 8 toothpicks

Instructions:

1. Cut the corn cobs in half so you have 8 half cobs of corn.

2. Insert a toothpick into one of the ends of each cob to produce a corn lollipop

3. Place the butter into a large saucepan and turn the pan on to a medium heat.

4. Meanwhile, heat another smaller saucepan on another element, and add the pistachio kernels to roast.

5. When the large pan is hot, add the corn cobs and brown on all sides until the corn is cooked (about 15 minutes)

6. Remove the pistachios from the other pan, and set on a place to cool

7. Once the pistachios are cool, roughly chip with a knife and add to a small serving bowl with the sour cream, salt pepper. Mix well to combine.

8. Remove the cooked corn from the pan and set onto a large serving platter

9. Use the pistachio cream to dip the corn into while eating.

Chili Con Carne

Ingredients:

- 500g beef mince
- 1 onion
- 1 clove garlic
- 2 Tbs extra virgin olive oil
- 1 tsp ground smoked or sweet paprika
- ¼ tsp nutmeg
- ¼ tsp ground coriander
- 3 shakes ground cardamom
- ½ tsp ground cumin
- ¼ tsp salt
- 3 shake chili flakes
- 1 400g tin crushed tomatoes
- 1 400g tin corn kernels
- 1 400g tin chili beans/white or black bean mix

- 1 cup white rice

Instructions:

Place a medium saucepan on the stove over a medium heat.

Place the rice into a pot on the stove and cover with 2 cups of hot water. Bring the pot to the boil and cook for 20-25 minutes.

Finely dice the onion and garlic, and place into the saucepan with the olive oil.

Brown the onion and garlic in the pan for about 5 minutes or until the onions are translucent and fragrant.

Turn the pan up to a high heat.

Add all of the beef mince to the pan and brown the mince for about 7 minutes.

Add all of the spices and salt to the pan and mix well to coat the mince.

Fry the spices with the mince for about 5 minutes.

Lastly, add the can of tomatoes, corn, beans and mix well to combine.

Turn the pan down to a low heat and simmer the mince for about 15 minutes until it becomes very soft and broken down.

Serve the rice in a bowl and spoon the mince on top and enjoy!

Beef nachos

Ingredients:

- 500g beef mince
- 1 onion
- 1 clove garlic
- 2 Tbs extra virgin olive oil
- 1 tsp ground smoked or sweet paprika
- ¼ tsp nutmeg
- ¼ tsp ground coriander
- 3 shakes ground cardamom
- ½ tsp ground cumin
- ¼ tsp salt

- 3 shake chili flakes
- 1 400g tin crushed tomatoes
- 1 packet nacho chips
- Sour cream
- Tomato salsa

Instructions:

Place a medium saucepan on the stove over a medium heat.

Finely dice the onion and garlic, and place into the saucepan with the olive oil.

Brown the onion and garlic in the pan for about 5 minutes or until the onions are translucent and fragrant.

Turn the pan up to a high heat.

Add all of the beef mince to the pan and brown the mince for about 7 minutes.

Add all of the spices and salt to the pan and mix well to coat the mince.

Fry the spices with the mince for about 5 minutes.

Lastly, add the can of tomatoes and mix well to combine.

Turn the pan down to a low heat and simmer the mince for about 15 minutes until it becomes very soft and broken down.

Serve the mince over a bed of the nacho chips, and garnish with a dollop of fresh sour cream and tomato salsa

Zesty Guacamole

Ingredients:

- 3 avocados
- Juice of 1 Lemon
- Zest of 1 lime
- 1 clove garlic

Instructions:

Spoon the contents of the avocados out into a small serving bowl

Crush the garlic through a garlic crusher and add to the avocado with the rest of the ingredients.

Mash the ingredients together with a fork until combined, with coarse chunks of avocado still remaining.

Serve this special guacamole with tortilla chips as a fancy Mexican-style entree.

Classic Mexican mince

Ingredients:

- 500g beef mince
- 1 onion
- 1 clove garlic
- 2 Tbs extra virgin olive oil
- 1 tsp ground smoked or sweet paprika
- ¼ tsp nutmeg
- ¼ tsp ground coriander
- 3 shakes ground cardamom
- ½ tsp ground cumin
- ¼ tsp salt
- 3 shake chili flakes
- 1 400g tin crushed tomatoes

Instructions:

Place a medium saucepan on the stove over a medium heat.

Finely dice the onion and garlic, and place into the saucepan with the olive oil.

Brown the onion and garlic in the pan for about 5 minutes or until the onions are translucent and fragrant.

Turn the pan up to a high heat.

Add all of the beef mince to the pan and brown the mince for about 7 minutes.

Add all of the spices and salt to the pan and mix well to coat the mince.

Fry the spices with the mince for about 5 minutes.

Lastly, add the can of tomatoes and mix well to combine.

Turn the pan down to a low heat and simmer the mince for about 15 minutes until it becomes very soft and broken down.

Chunky tomato salsa

Ingredients:

- 5 medium tomatoes
- ½ punnet yellow cherry or baby tomatoes
- ½ green capsicum
- 1 clove garlic
- 2 tsp white wine vinegar
- ½ tsp brown sugar
- 2 Tbs tomato paste
- 1 Tbs olive oil

Instructions:

Finely dice the tomatoes, cherry tomatoes, capsicum and garlic. Place all into a medium sized bowl.

Add the vinegar, brown sugar, tomato paste and olive oil to the vegetables and mix thoroughly with a spoon to evenly combine.

Serve the salsa with any Mexican dish or as an entree with tortilla chips and guacamole.

Fried chicken

Ingredients:

- 500g chicken breast or thigh
- 1 clove garlic
- 2 Tbs extra virgin olive oil
- 1 tsp ground smoked or sweet paprika
- ¼ tsp ground coriander
- ¼ tsp salt
- 1 cup panko crumbs (or breadcrumbs)
- 2 eggs

Instructions:

Place a medium saucepan on the stove over a medium heat.

Finely dice the onion and garlic, and place into the saucepan with the olive oil.

Brown the onion and garlic in the pan for about 5 minutes or until the onions are translucent and fragrant.

Turn the pan up to a high heat.

Whisk the two eggs in a small bowl and set aside.

Place the breadcrumbs into a small bowl.

Slice the chicken up into very thin strips then place each piece into first the egg, then into the breadcrumbs, coating each piece well.

Place the chicken into the hot pan and fry for about 15 minutes or until the crumbs are golden brown on the outside of the chicken pieces.

Enjoy the fried chicken dipping into salsa and sour cream!

Mexican pork tacos

Ingredients:

- 500g pork mince
- 1 onion
- 1 clove garlic
- 2 Tbs extra virgin olive oil
- 1 tsp ground smoked or sweet paprika
- ¼ tsp nutmeg
- ¼ tsp ground coriander
- 3 shakes ground cardamom
- ½ tsp ground cumin
- ¼ tsp salt
- 3 shake chili flakes
- 1 400g tin crushed tomatoes
- 1 packet nacho chips
- Sour cream
- Tomato salsa

Instructions:

Place a medium saucepan on the stove over a medium heat.

Finely dice the onion and garlic, and place into the saucepan with the olive oil.

Brown the onion and garlic in the pan for about 5 minutes or until the onions are translucent and fragrant.

Turn the pan up to a high heat.

Add all of the pork mince to the pan and brown the mince for about 7 minutes.

Add all of the spices and salt to the pan and mix well to coat the mince.

Fry the spices with the mince for about 5 minutes.

Lastly, add the can of tomatoes and mix well to combine.

Turn the pan down to a low heat and simmer the mince for about 15 minutes until it becomes very soft and broken down.

Serve the mince over a bed of the nacho chips, and garnish with a dollop of fresh sour cream and tomato salsa.

Nacho 'mess' bake

Ingredients:

- 500g beef mince
- 1 onion
- 1 clove garlic
- 2 Tbs extra virgin olive oil
- 1 tsp ground smoked or sweet paprika
- ¼ tsp nutmeg
- ¼ tsp ground coriander
- 3 shakes ground cardamom
- ½ tsp ground cumin
- ¼ tsp salt
- 3 shake chili flakes
- 1 400g tin crushed tomatoes
- 1 packet nacho chips

- 1 cup grated cheese
- 1 tsp smoked paprika
- 2 spring onions
- Sour cream to serve

Instructions:

Place a medium saucepan on the stove over a medium heat.

Finely dice the onion and garlic, and place into the saucepan with the olive oil.

Brown the onion and garlic in the pan for about 5 minutes or until the onions are translucent and fragrant.

Turn the pan up to a high heat.

Add all of the beef mince to the pan and brown the mince for about 7 minutes.

Add all of the spices and salt to the pan and mix well to coat the mince.

Fry the spices with the mince for about 5 minutes.

Lastly, add the can of tomatoes and mix well to combine.

Turn the pan down to a low heat and simmer the mince for about 15 minutes until it becomes very soft and broken down.

Meanwhile, preheat the oven to 200 and line a large and deep baking tray with baking paper.

Once the mince has cooked for 15 minutes, place the nacho chips on the bottom of the baking tray, and top with all of the mince, and finally, the grated cheese.

Sprinkle the smoked paprika on top and place the baking tray into the oven to bake for 15 minutes, or until the cheese is melted and slightly golden.

Serve the nacho bake with fresh sour cream and eat with your fingers using the nacho chips as spoons!

Burrito bowls

Ingredients:

- 500g beef mince
- 1 onion
- 1 clove garlic
- 2 Tbs extra virgin olive oil
- 1 tsp ground smoked or sweet paprika
- ¼ tsp nutmeg
- ¼ tsp ground coriander
- 3 shakes ground cardamom
- ½ tsp ground cumin
- ¼ tsp salt
- 3 shake chili flakes
- 1 400g tin crushed tomatoes

- 1 carrot, grated
- Lettuce, finely chopped
- 1 avocado, sliced
- 1 cup grated cheese
- 1 packet burrito bowls

Instructions:

Place a medium saucepan on the stove over a medium heat.

Finely dice the onion and garlic, and place into the saucepan with the olive oil.

Brown the onion and garlic in the pan for about 5 minutes or until the onions are translucent and fragrant.

Turn the pan up to a high heat.

Add all of the beef mince to the pan and brown the mince for about 7 minutes.

Add all of the spices and salt to the pan and mix well to coat the mince.

Fry the spices with the mince for about 5 minutes.

Lastly, add the can of tomatoes and mix well to combine.

Turn the pan down to a low heat and simmer the mince for about 15 minutes until it becomes very soft and broken down.

Spoon some mince inside of a burrito bowl.

Grate the carrot and cheese, chop the lettuce and avocado and serve these vegetables on top of the mince in your burrito bowl and enjoy!

Seared rump steaks with salsa verde

Ingredients:

- 4-5 medium sized pieces of rump steak
- ⅓ cup pine nuts or cashews
- Bunch of fresh basil
- 5 Tbs extra virgin olive oil
- ¼ cup grated parmesan cheese

Instructions:

1. Place all of the ingredients (except for the steak) into a blender and pulse to create a pesto-like mixture (about 15 pulses)

2. Heat a large saucepan on the stove over a high heat, with a drizzle of olive oil

3. Grind salt and pepper over both sides of the steaks and pub this into the steaks to coat well.

4. Once the pan is hot, place the steaks into the pan and cook on each side for 4 minutes (this will give you medium-rare steaks, cook for 2 minutes extra on each side for medium cooked steaks)

5. Serve the steaks with the salsa verde spooned on top.

Burritos

Ingredients:

- 500g beef mince
- 1 onion
- 1 clove garlic
- 2 Tbs extra virgin olive oil
- 1 tsp ground smoked or sweet paprika
- ¼ tsp nutmeg
- ¼ tsp ground coriander
- 3 shakes ground cardamom
- ½ tsp ground cumin
- ¼ tsp salt
- 3 shake chili flakes
- 1 400g tin crushed tomatoes
- 1 carrot, grated
- Lettuce, finely chopped

- 1 avocado, sliced
- 1 cup grated cheese

Mince and spicy potato wedges

Ingredients:

- 500g beef mince
- 1 onion
- 1 clove garlic
- 2 Tbs extra virgin olive oil
- 1 tsp ground smoked or sweet paprika
- ¼ tsp nutmeg
- ¼ tsp ground coriander
- 3 shakes ground cardamom
- ½ tsp ground cumin
- ¼ tsp salt
- 3 shake chili flakes
- 1 400g tin crushed tomatoes
- 1 kg Dutch cream potatoes (or any waxy potato)

- ¼ tsp chili
- ¼ tsp salt
- ¼ tsp pepper
- ½ tsp dried oregano

Instructions:

Preheat the oven to 200°C and line the large baking tray with baking paper.

Wash the potatoes thoroughly in warm water but keep the skins on.

Slice each potato into wedges and layout on the baking tray flat.

Drizzle the potato wedges with the olive oil, and sprinkle over the second amount of chili, salt, pepper, and oregano.

Place the wedged into the oven for about 35 minutes or until golden brown and slightly crispy on the skin.

Meanwhile, place a medium saucepan on the stove over a medium heat.

Finely dice the onion and garlic, and place into the saucepan with the olive oil.

Brown the onion and garlic in the pan for about 5 minutes or until the onions are translucent and fragrant.

Turn the pan up to a high heat.

Add all of the beef mince to the pan and brown the mince for about 7 minutes.

Add all of the spices and salt to the pan and mix well to coat the mince.

Fry the spices with the mince for about 5 minutes.

Lastly, add the can of tomatoes and mix well to combine.

Turn the pan down to a low heat and simmer the mince for about 15 minutes until it becomes very soft and broken down.

Serve the mince over top of the hot wedges and use these to dip into the mince!